MARY McLEOD BETHUNE

The African-American Biographies Series

—African-American Biographies—

MARY McLEOD BETHUNE

Educator and Activist

Series Consultant:
Dr. Russell L. Adams, Chairman
Department of Afro-American Studies, Howard University

Andrea Broadwater

 Enslow Publishers, Inc.
40 Industrial Road   PO Box 38
Box 398   Aldershot
Berkeley Heights, NJ 07922   Hants GU12 6BP
USA   UK
http://www.enslow.com

This book is dedicated to my parents.

Library of Congress Cataloging-in-Publication Data

Broadwater, Andrea.
    Mary McLeod Bethune: educator and activist / Andrea Broadwater.
       p. cm. — (African-American biographies)
    Summary: Traces the life and achievements of the black educator who fought bigotry and sought equality for blacks in the areas of education and political rights.
    Includes bibliographical references and index.
    ISBN 0-7660-1771-0
    1. Bethune, Mary McLeod, 1875–1955—Juvenile literature. 2. African American women political activists—Biography—Juvenile literature. 3. African American women educators—Biography—Juvenile literature. 4. African American women social reformers—Biography—Juvenile literature. 5. African Americans—Biography—Juvenile literature. 6. African Americans—Civil rights—History—20th century—Juvenile literature. [1. Bethune, Mary McLeod, 1875–1955. 2. Teachers. 3. African Americans—Biography. 4. Women—Biography.] I. Title. II. Series.
    E185.97.B34 B76   2003
    370'.92—dc21

                             2002006827

Printed in the United States of America

10 9 8 7 6 5 4 3 2 1

To Our Readers: We have done our best to make sure all Internet Addresses in this book were active and appropriate when we went to press. However, the author and the publisher have no control over and assume no liability for the material available on those Internet sites or on other Web sites they may link to. Any comments or suggestions can be sent by e-mail to comments@enslow.com or to the address on the back cover.

Every effort has been made to locate all copyright holders of material used in this book. If any errors or omissions have occurred, corrections will be made in future editions of this book.

Illustration Credits: Florida State Archives, pp. 8, 16, 19, 38, 41, 45, 48, 51, 61; Library of Congress, pp. 12, 22, 35 (both), 58, 78, 85, 91, 93; Moody Bible Institute, p. 28; Moorland-Spingarn Research Center, Howard University, p. 53; National Archives, p. 69; National Park Service—Mary McLeod Bethune Council House NHS, Washington, DC, p. 97; Schomburg Center for Research in Black Culture with permission from the Archives Center, National Museum of American History, p. 73.

Cover Illustration: National Park Service—Mary McLeod Bethune Council House NHS, Washington, DC.

CONTENTS

Acknowledgments

I would like to thank the following
for their invaluable assistance:

The Harlem Writers Guild

Schomburg Center for Research in Black Culture
The New York Public Library

1

"BUT WE VOTED!"

he meeting took place behind drawn curtains. The participants spoke in hushed tones. Mary McLeod Bethune, founder and president of the Daytona Normal and Industrial Institute, warned the group, "Use your minds, but keep your lips closed."[1]

What was the reason for this gathering shrouded in secrecy? It was the upcoming mayoral election in Daytona Beach, Florida. Although the Constitution grants every United States citizen the right to vote, the people at this meeting had never been permitted to exercise this right. All those in attendance were United

Mary McLeod Bethune

States citizens—but they were also African Americans in the year 1920.

At that time, African Americans faced threats, intimidation, and even death if they attempted to vote. The upcoming election involved an important issue for the people who had gathered that night: At stake was a proposed bill for the first public high school for black students. The candidate who opposed it was backed by the hate group Ku Klux Klan (KKK). The other candidate, who supported the bill, had promised also to improve conditions in the black community with better streets, lighting, and sewers.

These issues were very important to Bethune. Thanks to her unrelenting efforts, the Daytona Institute had grown from a small cottage to a multiple-building campus. There, she educated young blacks through the eighth grade. The African-American community had supported Bethune's school financially and in other ways as well. Bethune, in turn, played a big role in the education and general welfare of the community. Her involvement in civic organizations such as African-American women's clubs and the Red Cross also made her a well-respected figure.

Bethune had taken on many projects to ensure racial progress. This election was one of them. The recent Nineteenth Amendment to the Constitution gave women the right to vote. Bethune rang doorbells and urged African Americans, especially women, to register. She insisted that her school faculty register to vote. But she also warned everyone about the tactics that the white community had invented to prevent blacks from registering. African Americans—who lacked the opportunities for schooling—were told they must pass a literacy test. Few of them could read or write, so few could pass the test. Another effective means of blocking African Americans from voting was the poll tax. The fee of $1 or $2 was more than many of them could afford.

Bethune was undaunted. This election was too important. She urged the members of the African-American community to pay the poll tax even if it meant doing without other things.

Meanwhile, Bethune's efforts were not going unnoticed by the treacherous Ku Klux Klan. Bethune received a warning that the Klan was planning to take action against her. Such a threat would have terrified an ordinary person. The white supremacist Klan, founded in Tennessee in 1866, had set out on a vicious campaign to maintain white control of the South. The KKK sought to prevent African Americans, not long out of slavery, from taking advantage of their new opportunities. The Klan used tactics such as cross burnings and lynchings—the murder of innocent people by lawless mobs—to spread terror throughout the South.

Despite the long, violent history of the Klan,

Bethune was steadfast in her faith. She believed that when the Klan arrived, God would guide her. She had faced up to the Klan in her earlier days in Daytona Beach. She knew that anyone—black or white—who attempted to improve conditions for black people risked becoming the Klan's target.

On the eve of the election, Bethune heard horses' hooves approaching the Daytona Institute. Through its political connections, the Klan had arranged to have all the street lamps turned off. When Bethune looked out the window, she saw a herd of hooded riders approaching through the darkness. She was ready for them.

One hundred Klansmen guided their horses through the campus gate and surrounded the main building, Faith Hall. Bethune immediately ordered her frightened students to turn off all the lights in the building. The Klan did not control the school's lights, and she next ordered all the campus lights turned on. "Let them know we're home!" she said.[2] Her students were now shielded by darkness while the Klansmen stood in brightness.

The spectacle caused one young girl to scream in terror. Other students began to wail. Then an older girl remembered a hymn she had learned. "Be not dismayed whate'er betide," she sang aloud. "God will take care of you." Some of the other students began to join in. As the chorus emanated from Faith Hall, the hooded

Members of the Ku Klux Klan taught hatred to their children. Hidden behind white hoods, the Klansmen terrorized the South.

men turned their horses around and galloped away. They had failed to intimidate Bethune and the students.

At 8:00 A.M. on Election Day, Bethune and her staff arrived at the voting polls. There they found two lines, one for black voters and the other for white voters. Those in the long, unmoving line of black voters watched as all the whites were invited in to vote. Bethune walked up and down, encouraging her people to stay and exercise their right to vote.

Just before closing time, after every white person had voted, the blacks were allowed inside. The next day Bethune declared, "They kept us waiting all day, but *we voted!*"[3] To add to her victorious stand against the Klan, the candidate she favored won the election.

This would be only one of many triumphs for the brave woman born to former slaves in Mayesville, South Carolina.

2

THE GIRL WHO WANTED TO READ

other worked in the fields at Father's side,"
said Mary McLeod Bethune about her
parents.[1] Samuel McLeod and Patsy
McIntosh McLeod were her early models of hard work
and determination. Samuel McLeod also practiced
various trades such as carpentry and leather work.
Patsy McIntosh McLeod worked as a cook and
midwife. She had grown up near Mayesville, South
Carolina, not far from where Samuel McLeod lived.
They met and eventually wanted to marry and have a
family. However, it was the nineteenth century before

emancipation—and Patsy McIntosh and Samuel McLeod were slaves.

Since the 1700s, millions of Africans had been brought to the United States against their will. These human beings were bought by slave owners and forced to work for free, often under the brutal lash of the whip. They were stripped not just of their freedom but also of their language, religion, culture, and even their names. Thus Samuel McLeod was named after his owner, McLeod, and Patsy McIntosh was named after her owner, McIntosh.

Despite this inhumane treatment, slaves struggled to maintain the basic social structure, the family. Many slaves lived in long unions even though their owners did not permit them to legally marry.[2] Samuel McLeod's owner, however, agreed to purchase Patsy McIntosh so the couple could marry and be together.

After their marriage, Samuel and Patsy both worked on the McLeod cotton plantation. They had many children, though the slave owner sold several of them to nearby plantation owners. Other slaves who passed through on errands would report back to Samuel and Patsy on the welfare of their children.

In 1865, the defeat of the South in the Civil War ended slavery. The McLeods and their children were freed. Many slave owners feared retribution from their slaves, but the McLeods were not focused on revenge.

Mary's parents, Samuel and Patsy McLeod, spent many years of their lives in slavery.

They had the same intent as most other newly freed slaves. They wanted to build a life as free people.[3]

Like many others who had been slaves, the McLeods continued to work for their former owners. They saved money from their wages until they had enough to buy five acres of hilly land near Mayesville. Samuel and their older sons cut down trees and built a log cabin that they named the "Homestead." Some of their children who had been sold years earlier returned after emancipation to live there.

The McLeod family continued to grow. Patsy and Samuel's fifteenth child was born on July 10, 1875, in the Homestead. They named their new daughter Mary Jane.

Unlike her older brothers and sisters, Mary Jane was born free. Patsy McLeod said that Mary Jane was different in other ways, too. Mary Jane always wanted to share her things with other children. She did not care for some of the foods and drinks that her brothers and sisters enjoyed, such as grape wine.

As a youngster, Mary Jane often listened to her parents and older brothers and sisters talk about slavery. She paid close attention to the stories of Grandmother Sophia, who smoked a corncob pipe and told of the beatings she had received as a slave. Very religious, Grandmother Sophia would sit by the fireplace and speak as if God were right there in the room. She would say things like, "Dear God, I am so happy to be living in this loving family circle. I'm sitting here in my chimney corner eating preserves and hot biscuits with butter in them and having good things without having to count the lashes that bring blood trickling down your back."[4] She was recalling the beatings she had received as a slave.

The McLeods held family prayer sessions every morning and evening. Mary Jane learned Bible stories from her mother and grandmother. Slaves had been forbidden to learn how to read or write, but they told

Bible stories. Sometimes a visiting preacher read the Bible to them.

Their strong faith helped the McLeods endure the difficult times that befell them even after slavery. The family worked in the rice and cotton fields under the scorching sun. Young Mary Jane rode their mule, Old Bush, in the fields. By the age of nine, she could pick 250 pounds of cotton a day.

The children also had household chores. The Homestead had a large family room and two smaller bedrooms. Mary Jane swept the dirt floors until they looked polished. Samuel McLeod had built shelves along the walls for beds. Patsy stuffed sacks with tree moss for mattresses. She also cured meats and stored preserves away for winter. Sometimes neighbors would come to borrow food. Some were white farmers who had lost possessions during the war. Patsy always shared what little she had.

Patsy McLeod also worked as a midwife, helping women give birth. Mary Jane would accompany her mother with a lantern at night. Patsy McLeod delivered the babies and accepted what little, if any, the families could pay.

One day, Mary Jane was helping her mother return some laundered clothes to her former slave mistress. Mary Jane stopped to play with the white children of the house. Among their playthings, she spotted a book. When Mary Jane picked it up, the little girl said

Two of Mary's sisters, Rachel and Maria, stand in front of the Homestead, the family's log cabin.

to her, "You can't read that. Put that down."[5] In those days, white people believed that blacks did not have the mental ability to learn to read, and it was against the law to teach them.

The child's words struck Mary Jane. She promised herself that she would learn to read one day. Later, she stated that the white girl's words made her see the importance of education. She thought that maybe the reason white people had better homes and a better lifestyle was a matter of reading and writing.[6]

This new awareness followed Mary Jane everywhere. She prayed for the chance to go to school and learn how to read. One day, she accompanied her father to the gin mill, where cotton was weighed and sold. The man who owned the mill weighed her father's cotton and told him that it came to about 250 pounds. Mary Jane thought that if she had been educated, she could figure how much it weighed.[7]

Mary Jane often went along on her father's business errands. One day, Samuel McLeod took his daughter to the market in Mayesville. The trip was a treat for her birthday. It was near the Fourth of July, and the holiday festivities included a rodeo. The town crowd, segregated by race, stood around in a fun mood. Some were drinking, and one of the white men spotted a man in the black section as a good target for troublemaking. He lit a match and shoved it under the black man's nose. Flinging out his arms in surprise, the black man accidentally knocked the white man to the ground. Instantly, the festive mood ended. The black man had made a dangerous mistake. Any such act against a white person by a black person often resulted in death. Samuel McLeod grabbed Mary Jane and told her not to look back. As they hurried away, they heard cries for a lynching. Later that night, Mary Jane could hear her parents speaking in low tones about what had happened that day.

Mary Jane held fast to her faith and continued to pray to go to school. One day her prayers were answered in the appearance of Miss Emma Jane Wilson. The Board of Missions for Freedmen of the

Presbyterian Church had sent Miss Wilson to open a school for the children of former slaves.

Miss Wilson was the first light-skinned African American Mary Jane had ever seen. She was also the first African-American woman Mary Jane had heard addressed as Miss. In the South, African Americans were not given the respect of titles such as mister or miss.

The McLeods could spare their children from the fields for only a few months of the year. Mary Jane eagerly jumped at the opportunity to go to Miss Wilson's school. With a lunch pail and slate that her father bought, Mary Jane walked five miles to the one-room schoolhouse. Miss Wilson met the children at the door of the Mayesville Institute. Bethune later described her first day: "The first morning she was standing at the door and greeted us so pleasantly that we all felt easy, all these crude and crudely dressed boys and girls from the South Carolina rurals."[8]

Mary Jane pursued her study at the mission school despite attempts to stop her. Often she had to walk past taunting white children who would throw rocks or send a dog chasing after her. But Mary Jane was undeterred. She did what others said she could not do: She learned to read. Now she could read the Bible to her family, which made her mother and grandmother very proud. Mary Jane went as far as she could in the Mayesville Institute.

She also still worked in the fields with her family. On one of her trips to the cotton gin with her father, she watched the cotton hoisted up to be measured. The owner told her father that he had 280 pounds. This time Mary Jane studied the scales and figured out the weight. "Isn't it 480 pounds?" she asked the owner.[9] He told her that she was right. After that, other farmers—black and white—asked her to do figures for them.

When the Reverend J. W. E. Bowen of Atlanta,

Like these pickers, Mary Jane worked all day long in the cotton fields.

Georgia, passed through the town, the McLeod family went to hear him. The preacher spoke about the people in Africa. He said that missionaries needed to go to Africa and preach the Christian faith. His sermon inspired Mary Jane. She resolved to become a missionary in Africa.[10] She also prayed to be able to continue her studies.

This time her prayer was answered through a white teacher in Denver, Colorado. The teacher, Mary Chrisman, also worked part time as a seamstress. Inspired to charity by a leaflet from the Presbyterian mission board, Chrisman donated her extra money to pay for a black girl to attend Scotia Seminary in Concord, North Carolina. Mary Jane was selected for this extraordinary opportunity. Her teacher, Miss Wilson, a graduate of Scotia Seminary, delivered the good news.

The entire community rejoiced that one of their own would go on to higher learning. Some of their neighbors assisted the McLeod family by knitting clothing for Mary Jane. Her mother also altered dresses for her to take. Her father bought a trunk for her trip.

When Mary Jane McLeod left for Scotia Seminary in 1887, everyone in the community stopped work. They walked or rode on oxcarts to the Mayesville train station and watched their Mary Jane board the train for a brand-new world.

3

A NEW MISSION

ary Jane McLeod arrived at Scotia Seminary in Concord, North Carolina, in the fall of 1887. She knew that she had entered a whole new world when she saw the brick buildings with their stairways and glass windows. At dinner, the table was set with water glasses and a variety of cutlery. Not sure which knife or fork to use, she watched how the other students ate.[1]

At the head of the table sat Dr. David Satterfield, the school's white principal. The teachers—black and white—sat at the table together. This was an unusual sight to a girl who had lived her whole life in the segregated South.

Many white northern Presbyterians taught at the school, bringing their views of racial equality. Mary Jane saw blacks and whites working and eating together amicably. This interracial experience served as a model for her in the future.

Many of the girls had come from North Carolina cities such as Raleigh and Charlotte. Despite her rural background, Mary Jane made friends easily. She became a leader among the girls and was not afraid to speak to school administrators on the students' behalf. Her sense of responsibility won her the assignment of bell ringer for the school's schedule.

One time, though, when Mary Jane was in a hurry, she failed to act responsibly. As she rushed down the stairs, she ran straight into the school principal. Dr. Satterfield sternly reprimanded Mary Jane and gave her three demerits. After fifteen demerits, a girl would be sent home. In his office, Mary Jane tearfully apologized. Dr. Satterfield lectured her on how her behavior reflected on her race and said she should always set an example.

The program at the Scotia Seminary focused on educating the whole student, "For Head, Hand and Heart."[2] Mary Jane's academic classes included English, Latin, history, and mathematics. She also studied music. Her music teacher, Miss Ida Cathcart, gave her extra attention because of her good singing voice.

In 1890, Mary Jane graduated to the Normal and Scientific Course. This program was the equivalent of today's junior college. Students who completed this course of study were certified as teachers.

Religion was also an important part of Mary Jane's life. A second building, Faith Hall, was added to the campus. Mary Jane often worshiped in its chapel.

From working in the kitchen to scrubbing the stairs, Mary Jane's daily chores occupied her hands as well. She could not afford to return home during summer vacations, so Mrs. Satterfield found work for her with white families. Mary Jane tended to their children or did farm chores.

The McLeod family was going through hard times. Their mule, Old Bush, had died, and Mary Jane's father had to mortgage the farm. This meant that he had to use the value of his farm to secure a loan from the bank. Often farmers could not pay off their mortgages, and the banks took ownership of their farms.

So despite having little money for herself, Mary Jane sent money back home to her family whenever she could. At one point, she had only one blouse to wear. She washed it every night so it would be clean the next day. She did this until the missionary barrels arrived. These were filled with secondhand clothes sent through the church missions. The girls would open the seams and use the fabric to make themselves new dresses.

When Mary Jane graduated from Scotia Seminary in June 1894, though, she wore a white dress made from new material donated by Miss Cathcart. It was a proud and happy time. Shortly before graduation, she was summoned to Dr. Satterfield's office. He and Mrs. Satterfield greeted her with wonderful news about her wish to become a missionary in Africa. With Dr. Satterfield's assistance, she had applied to the mission training school of the Moody Bible Institute in Chicago, Illinois. Mary Jane had been accepted, and Miss Chrisman, her previous benefactor, again agreed to pay her tuition. Her parents could not afford even to attend the graduation ceremony at Scotia Seminary.

In July 1894, Mary Jane McLeod traveled to Chicago to begin the two-year program at the Moody Bible Institute. Again she found herself in a whole new world, the only African American among one thousand students.

As McLeod knelt to pray, her roommate expressed surprise to see the light soles of her feet. The nineteen-year-old responded lightheartedly that her palms were light as well.[3] In spite of comments like this, it did not take long for McLeod to adapt to her new surroundings. The other students extended themselves to make her comfortable. She later stated that at the Moody

Students from the Moody Bible Institute carried their religious fervor into the streets. They rode through Chicago in "gospel wagons" to share their faith.

Bible Institute, she learned "a love for the whole human race regardless of creed, class, or color."[4]

Mary Jane McLeod's faith deepened at the school. The institute trained its students to be evangelists, preaching the Christian faith in the streets of Chicago. McLeod also sang in the choir. She visited local police stations and sang to those behind bars. The students also knocked on doors in various neighborhoods to tell the residents about the services at the school.

During one of these trips, McLeod had a frightening experience. A young woman invited her in. Entering a room filled with men and women in a raucous mood, McLeod began to read from a religious tract about sin. Her words amused the revelers, who had obviously been drinking. She decided to leave but discovered that the door was locked. As the group's laughter grew, McLeod just prayed. Finally, someone opened the door and McLeod hurried home in the dark.

McLeod also had the opportunity to travel even farther to evangelize. For a special spring project, the students traveled in the midwestern states to establish Sunday schools. During the trip, McLeod stayed at a white family's home in South Dakota.

At the Moody Bible Institute, McLeod grew into a self-assured young woman. Nearing the end of her study there, she confidently applied to the Mission

Board of the Presbyterian Church for an assignment in Africa.

Unfortunately, the board quickly dashed her long-held hopes, informing her that there were no positions available for an African-American missionary. McLeod later said that she was "greatly disappointed" by the rejection.[5]

So McLeod returned to her hometown. For a year, she assisted her former teacher Miss Emma Wilson at the Mayesville Institute. Then she applied to the Presbyterian Board of Education for a teaching position and was assigned to the Haines Normal and Industrial Institute in Augusta, Georgia.

The institute had been founded by Lucy Craft Laney, a well-known African-American educator. Laney, the first woman to graduate from Atlanta University, opened the Haines Institute to educate African-American girls, but eventually the school began to accept boys as well. The Haines Institute prepared students to become teachers or to go on to college. Laney also developed the first kindergarten in Augusta. The Haines Institute was the only school at that time founded by a woman that became comparable in scale to the famed Tuskegee Institute.

Mary Jane McLeod taught eighth grade. The school was in a poverty-stricken area, and she reached out into the community with her missionary zeal. McLeod persuaded the parents to send their children to the Haines Institute Sunday school. She and her students bathed the children and dressed them in clothing from the missionary barrels. Under McLeod's direction, Sunday school attendance grew to a thousand children.

The dynamic Laney greatly influenced McLeod. McLeod later stated that because of her experience at the Haines Institute, she discovered her new mission: "My life work lay not in Africa, but in my own country."[6]

In 1897, McLeod transferred to another teaching position, at the Kindell Institute in Sumter, South Carolina. There, life held a different kind of lesson for the young teacher—a lesson for the heart.

4

HEAD, HAND, AND HEART

Singing in the choir at the Kindell Institute, McLeod met a handsome young fellow teacher, Albertus Bethune. After graduating from Avery Institute in Charleston, North Carolina, Bethune had worked as a schoolteacher. After a while, though, he left teaching, hoping to earn more money in business. He now worked as a salesman in the men's clothing section of a department store.

Love swiftly swept McLeod off her feet. After a whirlwind courtship, they married in 1898, then moved to Savannah, Georgia, where Albertus was offered another job selling men's clothing. In 1899, their only child, Albert McLeod Bethune, was born. Mary Jane took off a year to tend to her baby. Yet the desire to build a school for black girls burned in her soul. She later said, "This married life was not intended to impede things I had in mind to do. The birth of my baby boy had no tendency whatever to dim my ardor and determination."[1]

A pastor from Palatka, Florida, invited Mary Jane Bethune to open a mission school there, and she accepted. With her nine-month-old son, Bethune moved to Palatka. Her husband later joined her and found a job there. Still, his income and her teacher's salary were not enough to support the young family. So in addition to teaching at the school, Mary Jane sold policies for the Afro-American Life Insurance Company. Her part-time sales work for various insurance companies would provide income for her through the years.

After several years at the Palatka school, Bethune set off again. Albertus did not share her passion for education and advised her to stay in her current job.[2] But his words went unheeded. His wife's dream to start her own school had been fueled by a person she deeply admired: Booker T. Washington.

Washington, a former slave, had founded the Tuskegee Normal and Industrial Institute in Alabama. He preached a self-help philosophy for southern black farmers. He urged them to acquire land and learn how to cultivate it. Washington believed that blacks needed to learn practical trades like farming and carpentry. To this end, he developed a Department of Agriculture at the institute that had on staff the brilliant African-American scientist George Washington Carver. The Tuskegee Institute educated thousands of black farmers through conferences and fairs.[3] Bethune read the writings of Booker T. Washington, and they inspired her.

First Bethune needed to find a place to build her school. She had heard that Daytona Beach might be a good possibility. Black laborers had settled near there to work on the construction of the Florida East Coast Railroad. Their children needed a school. Also, the wealthy tourists who vacationed at the beautiful beach would be a good source of funding.

In 1904, with just $1.50 and her small son, Bethune journeyed to Daytona Beach, where she and Albert stayed at a friend's house. The situation in Daytona Beach could have discouraged her. The laborers and their families lived in severe poverty and were not much better off than they had been in slavery. Many people tried to dissuade Bethune. They warned her that the Ku Klux Klan committed violent acts against anyone who tried to improve the status of African Americans.

Bethune was steadfast in her plans. One night, she had a striking dream in which a big man rode up on a

Bethune was influenced by the ideas of two African-American leaders and educators: Booker T. Washington, left, and W. E. B. Du Bois.

horse near the Halifax River. Bethune told the man that she was trying to build her school. The man introduced himself as Booker T. Washington. Then he handed her a handkerchief with a large diamond. "Here, take this and build your school," he said and rode away.[4]

This was not the first time Bethune's dreams seemed to push her toward her goal. Encouraged by the vivid dream, Bethune set out to find a place for her school. On Oak Street, she saw a two-story cottage for sale. The owner agreed to rent it for $11 a month. She gave the man her $1.50 and persuaded him to wait until the end of the month for the rest.

Bethune planned to live on one floor with her son and use the other floor for her school. But a school needed more than just a building. What would the students sit on? How would they do their lessons? Bethune searched the neighborhood for other people's throwaways. A large barrel became her desk. Discarded crates would serve as chairs for the students. Charred pencils could be used for writing.

On October 3, 1904, Bethune realized her dream. The Daytona Normal and Industrial Institute for Negro Girls opened its doors. Bethune welcomed the small children at the door. Her first students were five little girls: Ruth, Lucille, Lena, Ana, and Celeste. Young Albert also attended until he transferred to the Haines Institute.

The school's tuition of 50 cents a week per student did not cover all the expenses. Bethune had to draw from whatever resources she could find. Many people in the African-American community supported her efforts. Local black churches took up collections for the school. Church members sold chicken dinners for special purposes, such as to pay a grocery bill.[5]

Bethune also sold homemade ice cream and sweet potato pies to the railroad workers. She raised money and found supplies wherever she could. She later wrote, "I haunted the city dump and the trash piles behind hotels, retrieving discarded linen and kitchen ware, cracked dishes, broken chairs, pieces of old lumber. Everything was scoured and mended. This was part of the training to salvage, to reconstruct, to make bricks without straw."[6]

Less than two years later, Bethune's school had 250 students. She never turned away a child, and she needed more space. Some children stayed overnight when their parents had to travel with their employers. Bethune and her staff picked Spanish moss from the surrounding trees, dried it, and stuffed it into sacks for mattresses. For her personal needs, she applied the same ingenuity and frugal means. She wore second-hand dresses that had been cut and altered in the school's dressmaking classes.

In time, it became too costly for the school to continue to pay rent every month. The Daytona Institute

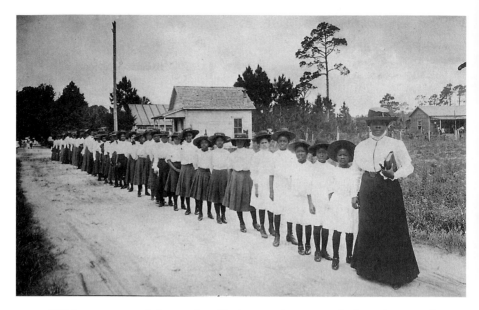

With energy and ingenuity, Bethune, above, made her dream of starting a school come true.

needed its own building. With her steadfast faith, Bethune set out to find some available land. In the black section of town was a garbage dump nicknamed "Hell's Hole." Bethune called the owner. Her request to buy the land surprised him, but he agreed to sell it to her for $200, with $5 down. Bethune hastened to raise the down payment. She sold ice cream and pies and hurried back with the coins gathered in her handkerchief.

Volunteers cleared the debris-strewn land. For the new building, Bethune begged for used bricks and other supplies. She also traded labor from the workmen for tuition for their families.

Bethune said that she knew that she would have to be a good beggar.[7] She would ride her old bicycle around town and ring doorbells for donations. A group of wealthy white women who belonged to the Palmetto Club often supported the school. Bethune later said that their help seemed to come when it was most needed. Much of the assistance, though, came from the wealthy men in Daytona Beach.

Bethune did not hesitate to ask for help. She gave talks at the local hotels. Sometimes she and the students sang for the hotel guests. If she read in a local newspaper of a wealthy vacationer in Daytona Beach, she would send a begging letter.

One such letter reached James Gamble of the Procter & Gamble Company. He agreed to see her and was quite surprised when she arrived at his home. Gamble had thought that a white woman was building the school.

Bethune asked Gamble to become a trustee of the school. He was surprised once again when he saw the makeshift classrooms. But Bethune's impassioned talk caused him to share her vision. Gamble became a trustee and donated legal services as well as financial assistance.

On one of her rounds, an elderly man recognized Bethune from a singing engagement. He introduced himself as Thomas H. White of Cleveland, Ohio. White, who had made a previous donation, asked to see the school. Bethune gave him a tour of the meager furnishings, which included a broken Singer sewing machine. White praised her efforts and wrote out a check for $200. Shortly after, he returned with more assistance, including an architect and some carpenters. In addition, he brought a brand-new sewing machine. Bethune had not known that White was the owner of the White Company, which manufactured White sewing machines.

White industrialists often donated money to schools for African Americans. Several foundations, such as the Peabody Fund and the Slater Fund, were established by philanthropists in the North. This was not just a simple good deed: These schools served their needs, too, by producing a skilled labor force and at the same time maintaining a segregated educational system.

The Slater Fund supported only schools that provided agricultural and industrial education. Many donors shared that policy. Often, schools for African Americans offered courses in agriculture, domestic science, and carpentry just so they could receive the badly needed funds.[8] Teaching these practical skills was in line with Booker T. Washington's philosophy.

On the other hand, some black leaders rejected this philosophy. The most well known of these was W. E. B. Du Bois, an African-American educator and a graduate of Harvard University. He believed that African

Americans should also study academic subjects such as literature and languages if they desired to do so. He insisted that African Americans could use their heads, not just their hands, to get ahead in life. Those who agreed with Du Bois were critical of Bethune and her emphasis on teaching vocational skills rather than intellectual pursuits.

Bethune was a practical woman. Throughout her life, she did whatever worked best for African Americans at the time. She admired Booker T. Washington's work at the Tuskegee Institute. Her southern background was similar to Washington's, and she believed that basic skills were necessary for black survival in the South. At the Daytona Institute, she taught her girls sewing, cooking, broom making,

Girls learned sewing and other practical skills at the Daytona Institute.

and other similar trades. They also learned about housekeeping, cleanliness, and dietetics. Like Booker T. Washington, Bethune was criticized by those who believed that skills training would not help African Americans improve their lives.

Still, Bethune also began adding academic courses as her school grew. This was in keeping with Du Bois's thinking. In 1907, the school's new building was dedicated. It was named Faith Hall after the building at Scotia Seminary. Etched over the entrance were the words "Enter to Learn." On the other side were the words "Depart to Serve."

Bethune later said that "Faith Hall was the first building given us by our Father in answer to our prayers, our faith, our works. Many homeless girls have been sheltered there and trained physically, mentally, and spiritually."[9]

This new building was just the beginning. Mary McLeod Bethune had much more in store for the Daytona Beach community.

5

BETHUNE-
COOKMAN COLLEGE

W here do I sit?" white visitors to Faith Hall would uneasily ask. Although unfinished, Faith Hall housed school and community meetings as well as religious services. The Sunday afternoon services, particularly the singing of the choir, attracted white guests, who then became supporters of the school. The state of Florida, like other southern states, enforced segregation laws known as "Jim Crow" laws. These were based on the 1896 Supreme Court decision in *Plessy* v. *Ferguson*. In this case, the Court ruled that public facilities could be racially segregated if they were "separate but equal."

As a result, many places set up separate black sections and white sections.

The Daytona Institute followed a different set of rules. Bethune would tell her guests to sit wherever they wished. She refused to abide by Jim Crow laws, even though other black schools did.[1]

Just as members of the community supported Bethune's school, the institute also reached out to the community. Five miles away, black laborers worked in a turpentine tree forest. Hired to tap the turpentine, the laborers and their families lived in work camps under deplorable conditions. After visiting the camps, located near the Tomako River, Bethune immediately sprang into action. In 1907, she established the Tomako Mission. The mission became a community project for her students. She and the students taught the residents Bible verses and how to read and write. They also taught the children games and songs and brought clothes from the missionary barrels.

Unfortunately, Bethune's professional success failed to carry over into her personal life. Albertus Bethune pursued his business ventures, including a horse-and-buggy taxi service. But he did not share his wife's educational commitments. In 1908, the Bethunes separated, with Albertus returning to his home state, North Carolina. The couple never reconciled.

Despite the breakup of her marriage, Mary

Bethune was always thinking about how to improve her school. She traveled far and wide to ask for donations.

McLeod Bethune forged on with her work. That year, 1908, the Daytona Institute was abuzz with a very important event: the visit of Booker T. Washington. A group including Washington and the director of the Slater Fund was touring black schools. Bethune saw to it that the campus was scrupulously cleaned for the special guests. Still, Faith Hall sat unfinished. The guests stayed in unplastered rooms and slept on borrowed linen. One guest commented on the dismal appearance. Booker T. Washington replied, "With a leader like Mrs. Bethune we don't know what may happen. Let's wait and see."[2]

Bethune sought funds for her school from near and far. In 1909, she traveled to New York to raise money. During her stay, she met Frances R. Keyser, a prominent African-American woman. Keyser was a graduate of Hunter College and the head of the White Rose Mission, an agency for troubled black girls. Bethune offered her a position at the Daytona Institute and Keyser accepted.

On Bethune's return trip, she stopped at the Hampton Institute in Virginia. The National Association of Colored Women (NACW) was holding a conference there. The NACW was composed of African-American women's clubs from across the country. Members included some of the brightest and best-educated women leaders of the race.

At the conference, Bethune met some women she

had long admired, including Mary Church Terrell, the NACW's first president, and Margaret Murray Washington, wife of Booker T. Washington. These older and more sophisticated women did not intimidate Bethune. She seized the opportunity to speak about her school, describing it with her usual eloquence and passion. Her talk so moved the elite group that they took up a collection for the Daytona Institute. After hearing young Bethune, Mary Church Terrell exclaimed, "She will some day be president of the National Association of Colored Women."[3]

The Daytona Institute continued to grow, especially with the addition of Keyser to the staff. Keyser assumed responsibility for the educational program. Bethune then could focus on the administration of the school. She also hired Portia Smiley, a graduate of Hampton Institute and of Pratt Institute in New York. Smiley instructed the students in handcrafts such as basketry, weaving, and beadwork. Often they sold their crafts at annual fairs and bazaars and raised considerable funds.

By 1911, many students had completed the eighth grade at Daytona Institute. Bethune approached the board of trustees with her desire to have the school accredited as a high school as well. She received a surprising response. She was told that an eighth-grade education was enough for black children.

Bethune insisted that black children deserved the

same opportunities as white children. She adamantly declared, "If you're going to tie my hands, I'll start over!"[4] However, she had one main supporter on the trustee board: James Gamble. Eventually, a high school program was developed at the school.

In 1911, another major development occurred as a result of Bethune's unrelenting struggle for her students. A student became acutely ill with appendicitis, and Bethune persuaded a white physician to admit the child for surgery at a whites-only hospital. When Bethune came to visit the girl, the receptionist ordered

Bethune, center, helps with a cooking class. The students learned how to plan and cook nutritious meals.

her to the back door. Bethune ignored her and strode into the hospital. Inside, she saw that the girl had been relegated to the back porch. Bethune later said, "Even my toes clenched with rage."[5]

Once again, Bethune met adversity with action. With help, she purchased a cottage located behind her school. The little cottage became a two-bed hospital supervised by Dr. T. A. Adams, the local black physician. Eventually, it was expanded into a two-story, twenty-six-bed facility that served the community. Named the Patsy McLeod Hospital after Bethune's mother, it also served as a training school for nursing students. Years later, to ease its financial burden, the Daytona Institute turned it over to the city of Daytona Beach.

In 1914, World War I broke out. Bethune received an unexpected telegram summoning her to Washington, D.C. Bethune had been recommended to give a speech on the issue of African-American participation in the Red Cross. Totally unprepared for such an occasion, she had to dig deeply into the missionary barrels to pull together an outfit. She even culled parts from two old hats to make a presentable one.

Bethune's wardrobe may have been makeshift, but her presentation was flawless. She spoke persuasively for African Americans' equal involvement in the Red Cross. As a result of her speech, she was sent on a three-state recruiting tour for the Red Cross. African

Americans became fully integrated into all areas of the Red Cross.

In Daytona Beach, the Red Cross held a rally at the Daytona Institute. Distinguished guests such as the governor of Florida and the U.S. vice president Thomas Marshall impressed many members of the community who had been reluctant to support the school.

In 1915, the first class graduated from the school. A new administration building, White Hall, was erected and named after one of the institute's staunch supporters, Thomas H. White. The school had grown academically as well. By 1916, it offered a standard high school curriculum. The courses of study included teaching, business, and nursing.

In 1919, Albertus Bethune died after a bout with tuberculosis. Mary McLeod Bethune never remarried. Instead, she concentrated on her work. Her primary concerns meshed with the emerging black women's movement of the time, which focused mainly on the education and uplifting of the race.[6]

In 1920, Bethune led the voter registration drive that caused the showdown between her and the Ku Klux Klan. When the KKK mob tried to intimidate her, Bethune showed her mettle—dousing the lights in Faith Hall and spotlighting the angry Klansmen outside. They retreated without doing any harm,

Bethune's school attracted many students, and its reputation for excellence grew. After a while, academic subjects were added to the course list.

and the candidate that Bethune supported won the election.

Also in 1920, Bethune was elected president of the Florida Federation of Colored Women's Clubs. Her major issue became the lack of facilities for troubled black girls. The state of Florida maintained a state prison for adult criminals and a residence for female white juvenile delinquents. On September 20, 1921, the Florida Federation of Colored Women's Clubs established a residence for black girls. Bethune used her own resources and fund-raising expertise to sustain the residence until it finally began receiving state funds.

For the Daytona Institute, Bethune persisted with her begging letters and doorbell ringing. Many people refused to help the school. Bethune stated, "If a prospect refused to make a contribution, I would say, 'Thank you for your time.' No matter how deep my hurt, I always smiled. I refused to be discouraged, for neither God nor man can use a discouraged person."[7]

Bethune gratefully accepted any donation no matter how small. Once, a man named J. S. Peabody gave her a contribution of 25 cents. Bethune thanked him and entered the sum in her record book. Two years later, they met again. When Peabody asked if she remembered his donation, Bethune looked it up in her notebook. Her diligent bookkeeping impressed Peabody so much that he pulled out his checkbook and wrote a check for $250. Mr. Peabody, Bethune discovered, was a rich and generous man who gave large amounts of money to charity. He became an enthusiastic supporter of Bethune's school, donating funds for a variety of projects. When he died, he left the school $10,000 in his will.

Another surprise benefactor was a woman named Flora Curtis, who often bought vegetables from the school's farm. Curtis was a finicky customer and usually spent about 10 cents. But when she died, she willed

Bethune called many important people to ask for money for her school. Over the years she became an expert fund-raiser.

$80,000 to the school. In 1922, a new dormitory was erected and named Curtis Hall in her honor.

Despite such generous donations, the school still struggled financially. Bethune refused state aid. She feared that state control would open the door for state laws enforcing segregation, which she vehemently opposed. The Roman Catholic Church expressed interest in buying the school and running it, but Bethune wanted it to remain nondenominational.

Meanwhile, in Jacksonville, Florida, the Cookman Institute, a school for African-American boys, was having problems with a dwindling enrollment. A member of the board of education of the Methodist Church suggested a merger, which would allow Bethune to maintain control of the school's policies. In 1923, the two schools joined together into the Daytona-Cookman Collegiate Institute. Later, the name was changed to Bethune-Cookman College.

In 1924, Bethune became a member of the Commission on Interracial Cooperation. This organization of blacks and whites worked to improve conditions for poor citizens in the South. At the first meeting, Bethune proposed a resolution for better schools. The chairperson, a white woman, casually referred to the proposal as "Mary's amendment." Bethune rose and stated, "As a delegate from Florida, I must insist on respect of that sovereign. . . . I ask that it be entered on the record that the resolutions were presented by Mrs. Mary Bethune."[8]

In 1924, Mary Church Terrell's prophetic words came true: Bethune ran for the presidency of the National Association for Colored Women. She ran against Ida B. Wells-Barnett, a well-known antilynching activist. Nevertheless, Bethune won the presidency of the NACW, which now made her a national leader with a national platform.

6

THE BLACK ROSE

"Lifting as We Climb" was the motto of the National Association of Colored Women, and few women could have better symbolized it than Mary McLeod Bethune. The politically active organization addressed such issues as prison reform, antilynching legislation, and job training for women. As president of the ten-thousand-member organization, Bethune had progressed from founding a school for black girls to becoming a leader of black women. She ignited the NACW with her missionary zeal.

In May 1925, Bethune and other officers of the

NACW attended a conference of the International Council of Women. The NACW was involved in the conference through its membership in the National Council of Women (NCW). Of the thirty-eight organizations in the National Council of Women, the NACW was the only black group.

Prior to the conference, Bethune and her officers had insisted on nonsegregated seating. They refused to be seated apart from the white women. However, one evening the policy was not followed. The NACW members walked out of the event, publicly expressing their outrage at being humiliated before women from all over the world. The members of the National Council of Women reassured them that they could sit anywhere. Bethune and her associates returned to the conference and resumed their participation.[1]

With the dual responsibilities of presiding over both a college and a national organization, Bethune was carrying a heavy load. Some friends offered to send her on a vacation—a four-month tour of Europe. In May 1927, Bethune set sail for a rare opportunity for relaxation. She was warmly received in London. Lady Nancy Astor, the first woman member of the British Parliament, threw a garden party in her honor. Bethune went on a tour of the House of Commons, Buckingham Palace, and Westminster Abbey.

The group also visited Vatican City in Italy. There, they joined a large audience of people who had come

Bethune divided her time between her school and other important causes, such as equal rights for women and African Americans.

to see Pope Pius. When the pope passed Bethune, he uttered a few sentences in Latin. An attendant translated his words to Bethune: "Oh blessed art thou among women."[2]

Wherever she went, Bethune was greeted without the racial prejudice that shadowed her back in the United States. There was just one incident when some diners in a restaurant complained about eating alongside African Americans. The group was composed of white American tourists.

Bethune also visited Paris. She lingered in the Louvre, the famed art museum, and browsed in the famous Parisian fashion salons. Bethune no longer wore castoffs from the missionary barrels. In Paris, she bought a gown adorned with black fringe.

Bethune was a large woman with dark brown skin and African facial features. She did not possess the popular European standards of beauty, such as long straight hair and light skin. Still, she had unwavering pride in her appearance. Bethune described her mother as having royal African blood. Secure in her dark beauty, Bethune would say, "The night has its beauties and its strengths and its charms as well as the day."[3]

In Switzerland, another special moment awaited the African-American traveler. A hillside rose garden captured Bethune's attention. Roses of many different colors bloomed there. In their midst stood a rose she had never seen before: a rich, velvety black rose.

Bethune later stated, "I realized that the Red rose did not want to be the Black rose. The Black rose did not want to be the Yellow rose. Every Rose just wanted to be itself, have an opportunity to make that self the best self it's capable of becoming."[4] The presence of the beautiful black rose among the other roses became a symbol of humankind for her.

While touring in Switzerland, Bethune used a cane to assist her over the hilly land. She enjoyed using it, and a cane later became part of her daily attire. She liked it not so much for support as for style and even began to collect canes as a hobby. Bethune returned home with her treasured souvenirs and memories.

Later in 1927, Bethune's position in the National Council of Women earned her an invitation to a special luncheon. It was hosted by Eleanor Roosevelt, wife of the governor of New York, Franklin D. Roosevelt. She invited the leaders of the NCW to her home.

Bethune's presence as the only black guest caused apprehension among the southern women. Where would she sit? Sara Delano Roosevelt, the governor's mother, assessed the situation. She took Bethune by the arm and led her to the guest of honor's seat near the hostess. From that day on, Bethune and Sara Roosevelt shared a special friendship that eventually included Eleanor Roosevelt.

During Bethune's presidency of the NACW, she widened its scope to include an international agenda.

A lasting friendship grew between Bethune and Eleanor Roosevelt, left.

The organization sought to improve the status of women in the Philippines, Puerto Rico, Haiti, and Africa. To address its national and international issues, Bethune believed that the NACW needed its own headquarters in Washington, D.C. Previously, the NACW had worked out of the Washington, D.C., home of the late great human rights leader Frederick Douglass. Bethune agreed that it was important to maintain the Douglass home, but she said that it was essential for the NACW to acquire its own building. Despite opposition from other members, Bethune initiated a fund-raising campaign.

On July 31, 1928, Bethune attained her goal. A new brick building was dedicated as the national headquarters of the NACW. It was the first African-American organization established in Washington, D.C.

Bethune also held several civic positions back in Daytona. Her post as director of a local Red Cross chapter drew her into a natural tragedy. In September 1928, a devastating hurricane hit southern Florida. The hurricane hit hardest in the Everglades, where migrant workers lived in makeshift camps. Thousands of them died. Bethune supervised the rescue and relief efforts. She reported from the tragedy, "Negroes and whites alike are sharing in the losses of homes, friends, property, and indeed life. . . . We are so happy that we were able to help a little and to direct and organize so that efficient service might be rendered."[5] She later raised funds to aid in rebuilding the region.

Also in 1928, Bethune's last year as president of the NACW, she traveled to Los Angeles, California, where the organization was holding its annual meeting. While there, she also planned to see her benefactor, Mary Chrisman. Chrisman's modest donations had enabled Bethune to fulfill her dreams. The two women had corresponded with each other over the years, and at the doorway to Chrisman's home, they embraced in tears.

That evening at the convention, Bethune presented Chrisman with a bouquet of flowers. She expressed her gratitude to Chrisman for funding her education. Bethune said, "Invest in a human soul. Who knows? It might be a diamond in the rough."[6]

Not long after that meeting in Los Angeles, Bethune received an invitation from President Calvin Coolidge to attend a child welfare conference in Washington, D.C. Bethune was the only African American invited. The next year, 1929, Bethune participated in the National Commission for Child Welfare under the administration of President Herbert Hoover. Bethune made suggestions for federal funding of schools for African Americans. She also became a member of the Hoover Commission on Home Building and Home Ownership.

These visits to the nation's capital foretold the major political figure that Bethune would become.

7

NATIONAL
COUNCIL OF
NEGRO WOMEN

n 1929, the stock market crash plunged the United States into the Great Depression. It would become the worst economic time in the country's history, with mass unemployment, widespread hunger, homelessness, and hopelessness. And yet Bethune chose that year to scale another rung in her ladder to uplift the race. She announced plans to create a coalition of national black women's organizations.

Bethune saw an umbrella organization as a powerful force to fight for racial progress. She explained, "If I touch you with one finger, you will scarcely notice it.

If I tap you with two fingers, you will feel a light pressure. But if I pull all my fingers together into a fist, you will feel a mighty blow."[1]

In March 1930, Bethune called a meeting to initiate her project. The officers of the National Association of Colored Women were noticeably absent. Many members thought there were already enough black organizations for the limited available funds. Some African Americans also objected to an all-black coalition when the trend was heading toward inter-racial organizations. Events over the next few years eventually won them over to Bethune's point of view.

Since emancipation, thousands of innocent black people had been lynched in the South. About thirty lynchings occurred in 1930 alone. The details were well known because the mass media publicized the horrendous deeds, and the news traveled widely.

Bethune wanted to see an end to this savagery. Through her involvement in the Commission on Interracial Cooperation, Bethune was aware of the potential power of white women's organizations. She issued a challenge.

Bethune released a press statement demanding that white southern women exert their influence to end the racial violence.[2] Jessie Daniel Ames, one of the white leaders, responded to the call. She helped to form the Association of Southern Women for the Prevention of Lynching (ASWPL). The ASWPL condemned mob violence. It accused the mob participants—mostly white men—of using false rape charges to keep blacks and white women under their control. Thanks to the effectiveness of the ASWPL, mob violence decreased. Black leaders praised the organization.

In 1931, nine young black men were falsely accused of raping several white women in a train boxcar. When the case went to trial, the men were given lengthy jail terms by an all-white jury. The case drew national attention and outrage. The "Scottsboro boys," as they were called, received support from around the world. Strangely, the ASWPL remained silent on the issue.

Bethune continued to be recognized for her many achievements. In 1931, a leading journalist, Ida Tarbell, named her one of the fifty most influential women in America.

In 1932, Franklin Delano Roosevelt was elected president. Like many African Americans at the time, Bethune was registered as a Republican, which was the political party of Abraham Lincoln. Roosevelt, a Democrat, did not appeal to many African Americans at first. But his wife, Eleanor, was more liberal on social issues, and she drew support for her husband.

In 1933, the Costigan-Wagner bill was introduced in Congress. It called for federal intervention when local authorities failed to respond appropriately to mob violence. The legislation had many supporters, including the National Association for the Advancement of Colored People (NAACP), which had fought for antilynching legislation for years. First Lady Eleanor Roosevelt also supported passage of the bill. Surprisingly, a dissenting voice came from Jessie Daniel Ames, the white activist who had helped start the Association of Southern Women for the Prevention of Lynching. As a southerner, she said, she could not support federal intervention over states' rights.

The Great Depression brought money troubles to Bethune-Cookman College. Bethune wrote in a letter, "We are passing through the most severe test of our lives."[3] As president, she had to take drastic steps to sustain the college. In 1933, she canceled various athletic and social activities. She also reduced teacher salaries.

President Roosevelt had developed a program called the New Deal to bring about economic recovery. The Depression had created problems for the youth of the country, too. Of the 21 million young people ages sixteen to twenty-four, some 5 million were out of school and jobless. Roosevelt had established the National Youth Administration (NYA) to hire people in that age bracket for job training and work programs. Bethune was selected to serve on the National Advisory Committee of the NYA.

Bethune's noteworthy deeds were soon rewarded. In 1935, Bethune was awarded the prestigious Spingarn Medal from the NAACP. The Reverend

Adam Clayton Powell, Sr., of Harlem, New York, wrote to her, "It is a long way from the rice and cotton fields of South Carolina to this distinguished recognition, but you have made it in such a short span of years that I am afraid you are going to be arrested for breaking the speed limit."[4]

More accomplishments followed at a record-breaking pace. During this time, black organizations faced a dilemma: Should they integrate their efforts with those of other groups or reinforce their own institutions? In a dramatic move, the leading educator and activist W. E. B. Du Bois resigned from the NAACP because of its push for integration. Du Bois stated that African Americans advanced the furthest "working by and for themselves."[5]

Once again, Bethune based her stance on what she believed would best benefit African Americans. She had had a long history with interracial cooperation. Yet, in December 1935, at the founding meeting of the National Council of Negro Women (NCNW) in Harlem, New York, she stated, "We need an organization to open new doors for young women [so] when [it] speaks its power will be felt."[6] This time the leaders of the National Association of Colored Women were present. The members unanimously elected Bethune president of the National Council of Negro Women. Bethune suggested making NACW leader Mary Church Terrell a vice president as a gesture of unity.

In April 1936, the National Advisory Committee of the National Youth Administration held its first meeting at the White House. The purpose of the meeting was to present resolutions on the youth program. Bethune was to give a report on the participation of minorities in the program. This would be her first meeting with President Roosevelt. In her direct manner, she spoke of the importance of the program for black youth and their families. Bethune stated, "We are bringing life and spirit to these many thousands who for so long have been in darkness."[7] Her presentation moved the president to tears. Aubrey Williams, the administrator of the NYA, commended Bethune on her presentation.

Two weeks later, Bethune was summoned back to the White House. Aubrey Williams met her with the good news. Roosevelt had decided to set up within the NYA a new department, the Division of Minority Affairs—and he wanted Bethune to head it. At first she was

In 1936, President Franklin D. Roosevelt asked Bethune to help run a program for young people seeking jobs.

reluctant to take on another responsibility. But she realized that it could open the door for other black women. Bethune accepted the position and expressed her appreciation. President Roosevelt stated, "Mrs. Bethune is a great woman. I believe in her because she has her feet on the ground: not only on the ground, but in the deep down ploughed soil."[8]

By 1936, Bethune was head of Bethune-Cookman College, head of the Division of Negro Affairs of the NYA, and head of the National Council of Negro Women.

What would she head next?

8

BETHUNE AND THE BLACK CABINET

s director of the Division of Negro Affairs, Bethune became the first African-American woman to head a federal agency. On the grand scale of the federal government, it was a minor position. Yet Bethune, who had built a school from crates and splinters, saw the potential power in this appointment.

In August 1936, Bethune called a meeting of black advisers and officers in the Roosevelt administration. After black leaders had urged President Roosevelt to seek counsel from informed African Americans, advisers were appointed to various government departments. Bethune addressed these appointees in her Washington, D.C., home: "Let us forget the particular office each one of us holds. We must think in terms as a 'whole' for the greatest service of our people."[1]

The group called itself the Federal Council on Negro Affairs, but the press nicknamed it the Black Braintrust, or the Black Cabinet. Members of the Black Cabinet included Robert Weaver, director of the Integration of Negroes into the National Defense Program Division of the Office of Production Management; Lawrence Oxley, Division of Negro Labor of the Department of Labor; William H. Hastie, assistant solicitor in the Department of the Interior; Robert Vann, special assistant to the U.S. attorney general; and Frank Horne, adviser to the Federal Housing Administration (also uncle of the famed singer Lena Horne).

These sophisticated, college-educated young men deferred to the sixty-year-old, southern-bred Bethune. Her influence came largely from her friendship with First Lady Eleanor Roosevelt. In January 1937, the Black Cabinet sponsored the National Conference on the Problems of the Negro and Negro Youth with Mrs. Roosevelt's assistance. This first conference brought together African Americans from various religious, civic, and political organizations. The conference ended with recommendations for the federal government to increase opportunities for African Americans in employment, education, health, and housing, and to provide equal protection under the law.

The recommendations were published as the Blue Book. Copies of the Blue Book were presented to members of Congress and other governmental departments. Bethune personally delivered a copy to President Roosevelt. The black press asked her how he responded. Bethune stated that African Americans could depend upon the interest and sincerity of the president in his efforts to justify their confidence in him and his program.[2]

Bethune did not hesitate to call upon the president to demonstrate his sincerity. In 1937, a congressional committee attempted to eliminate the $100,000

President Roosevelt's African-American advisers were known as the "Black Cabinet." Bethune, center front, was the first African-American woman to run a federal agency.

higher-education fund of the National Youth Administration. Bethune requested an appointment with Roosevelt when she heard the news. Excitedly, Bethune urged him to stop the cuts: "Think what a terrible tragedy it would be for America. Negroes would be deprived of the leadership of skilled and trained members of their race!"[3]

Suddenly, Bethune realized what she was doing. She was so caught up in her plea that she was pointing her finger at the president's nose. Immediately, she apologized. Roosevelt stated that he understood her concern and he would see what he could do. Later that week, Congress voted to keep the NYA grant intact.

That same year, Bethune received an invitation to President Roosevelt's second inauguration, and she attended the ceremony.

During this time, Bethune was still president of the National Council of Negro Women. She always pushed for African-American women to be involved in all areas—national and international. She learned that the Nazi government of Germany was persecuting its Jewish citizens. In 1938, the NCNW communicated to Roosevelt its concern and desire to aid the Jewish people.

Also that year, the NCNW held a conference at the White House with the first lady's assistance. Its theme was "The Participation of Negro Women and Children in Federal Programs." Bethune called the conference "history making" because more than sixty African-American women had been invited to the White House to express their concerns on national affairs.[4]

By 1938, the Commission on Interracial Cooperation had been renamed the Southern Conference for Human Welfare (SCHW). President Roosevelt had stated that the South was the worst economic problem of the nation. The SCHW pinpointed the main cause of the problem: segregation. Ironically, at one SCHW meeting, in Birmingham, Alabama, local segregation laws prevailed. Police officers surrounded the room, ready to arrest anyone who disobeyed the local law: Blacks and whites could not sit together in the auditorium. The riot squad stood guard to ensure that the members of the interracial SCHW sat on opposite sides of the room. Only from these segregated seats would the black and white members be permitted to discuss integration.

Mary McLeod Bethune and Eleanor Roosevelt entered the meeting while engaged in a conversation. The first lady took a seat on the aisle, right next to Bethune. The members informed the first lady of the local law, explaining that her choice of seats could cause trouble. Mrs. Roosevelt moved her chair to the center of the aisle, where she sat throughout the meeting. She was not sitting in the black section—but she was not on the white side either.

In 1939, Bethune enlisted the aid of the first lady

for another problem. A $500,000 grant had been allocated for a 167-unit housing project for African Americans in Daytona Beach. The project was being stalled. Bethune notified Mrs. Roosevelt, who contacted the Federal Housing Administration. Soon the project was under way.

The Civil Service Commission had by then made Bethune's job an official civil service position. The Black Cabinet held its second conference in 1939. The members reviewed the progress of their previous recommendations. They condemned segregation in any new federal housing. Bethune declared, "Residential ghettos preserve our shameful racism in brick and mortar for generations to come."[5] Once again, their recommendations were distributed to President Roosevelt and to governmental agencies.

Bethune and the rest of the Black Cabinet faced this dilemma throughout their tenure. Should they push to end segregated facilities or to create equal facilities for African Americans? Segregation was the reality, and so was the suffering of African Americans. Conditions were worse for African Americans in the segregated South. Letters poured in to the NAACP describing incidents in which black people were threatened with harm and even death when they sought aid from relief agencies.[6]

Members of the Black Cabinet chose to focus on how New Deal programs could best reach African

Americans. As always, Bethune was practical: "In places where there is no need for a separate program for Negro and white groups, we most heartily recommend the one program," she said. "And in fields where it is necessary for us to have a separate program, we most heartily recommend a separate program, taking, of course, under advisement, the necessity of the proper leadership and guidance."[7]

Bethune believed that only African Americans could provide the proper leadership for black programs. African Americans would see to it that the programs included equal black participation. Bethune worked tirelessly to increase black involvement in the NYA. She pushed for black supervisors and black assistants in state agencies across the country. In one year, she traveled forty thousand miles across twenty-one states.

Bethune also remained involved in the struggle for equal rights. In Washington, D.C., she joined a picket line of protestors outside a drugstore that was part of a chain that refused to hire African Americans. Bethune was fond of saying, "The drums in Africa beat in my heart. I cannot rest while there is a single Negro boy or girl lacking a chance to prove his worth."[8]

In February 1940, First Lady Eleanor Roosevelt visited Bethune-Cookman College. This was a tremendous honor for Bethune and for her school. In the rain, Mrs. Roosevelt gave a speech before an

Despite being busy with many political and social issues, Bethune was always devoted to her students.

overflowing crowd at the school's thirty-fifth anniversary celebration.

Bethune's health was suffering under the constant demands of her many roles, including her most recent position as vice president of the NAACP. After a series of asthma attacks, she was advised to have a sinus operation. At Mrs. Roosevelt's arrangement, Bethune entered the all-white Johns Hopkins Hospital in Baltimore, Maryland, in April 1940.

There, Bethune saw even in her unfortunate situation an opportunity to further black progress. African-American physicians were not allowed to treat their patients in white hospitals. Only white doctors could work in these hospitals. Bethune requested that two prominent African-American physicians of Baltimore be permitted to observe her operation. She succeeded in opening yet another door: The two physicians were allowed to watch the procedure.

During her hospital stay, Bethune received flowers from Eleanor Roosevelt. She also received a check from John D. Rockefeller, which she promptly forwarded to her school.

Despite her high visibility in the national arena, Bethune continued to encounter racist treatment. On one occasion, a white elevator operator referred to her as "Auntie." Bethune responded by asking the man, which of her brother's children was he?

Still, these incidents did not slow Bethune's energy.

She persisted with her goal for black representation in National Youth Administration committees in the southern states. By 1941, the NYA had hired twenty-seven blacks to assist the state directors. This included all southern states except Mississippi. When she had visited Mississippi previously, she had helped to develop a plan for the employment and training for teachers in the black schools.

Bethune promoted higher education benefits, which included the Special Fund for Negroes. This fund helped students through work relief. It aided black colleges and provided librarians to high schools.

Bethune also wanted black colleges to be included in the Civilian Pilot Training Program. Six black colleges participated, including the Tuskegee Institute. African Americans as well as women entered aviation through this program. Their participation would soon prove essential. World War II was raging in Europe, and American involvement in the war was imminent. Bethune and the United States would prove to be indomitable forces.

9

"I LEAVE YOU LOVE"

I t is no empty boast when we say a Negro has never betrayed this country. It is a record we must keep. . . . We must not fail America and as Americans we must insist that America shall not fail us!"[1] Bethune spoke those words at the 1941 Third National Negro Conference. The theme of the conference was "The Negro and National Defense." U.S. defense industries were gearing up for war. Bethune, like many other African-American leaders, wanted African Americans to be employed in the factories and manufacturing plants of the defense industry.

Labor leader A. Philip Randolph called for a march on the nation's capital in the spring of 1941. More than one hundred thousand people were expected to participate in this peaceful protest against racial discrimination. Randolph, a graduate of Cookman Institute, had widespread supporters, including Bethune.

President Roosevelt did not want this march to take place. He feared it could lead to racial troubles and violence in Washington, D.C. He had enough on his hands with the nation heading for a war. The president met with Randolph, who agreed to call off the march if the president would sign an antidiscrimination order. On June 25, 1941, President Roosevelt signed Executive Order 8802. It said, in part, "There shall be no discrimination in the employment of workers in defense industries or government because of race, creed, color, or national origin."[2] The order also established the Fair Employment Practices Commission.

Despite these achievements, black leaders knew that they had to be watchdogs in the fight for racial equality. In October 1941, the War Department established an advisory committee—the Women's Interest Section—in its Bureau of Public Relations. African-American women, though, were excluded from the committee. As president of the National Council of Negro Women, Bethune responded emphatically. "We are anxious for you to know that we want to be and insist upon being considered a part of our American democracy, not something apart from it. . . . We are not blind to what is happening. We are not humiliated. We are incensed!" she wrote in an open letter to Secretary of War Henry L. Stimson.[3]

With Eleanor Roosevelt's intervention, the NCNW joined the Women's Interest Section. African-American women now had a link to the War Department—and not a moment too soon. On December 7, 1941, Japan bombed the U. S. naval base in Pearl Harbor, Hawaii. The United States entered World War II.

In 1942, the National Youth Administration was threatened with elimination. Members of Congress wanted the funds reallocated to the war effort. The Senate overruled the Appropriations Committee and saved the NYA—at least for another year.

The NYA changed from a state-based system to a regional one. Under this new structure, the NYA hired black assistants in nine of its eleven offices. This revised system helped to produce work-skills training for black youth. During this time, Bethune fought for training in areas other than domestic and service occupations. These changes began to be realized through the war efforts. For example, in Wilberforce, Ohio, through a War Production Training Project, 350 black youths gained skills in machine shop, sheet metal, and radio and auto mechanics. The successful project became a symbol of black youth in the war-training phase of the NYA.[4]

Secretary of War Stimson appointed Bethune as special assistant to Lieutenant Colonel Oveta Culp Hobby, commanding officer of the Women's Army Auxiliary Corps (WAAC). Bethune succeeded in persuading Hobby and other officials to allot 10 percent of the WAAC officer class to African Americans. Bethune also participated in the selection of African-American women for Officers Training School at Fort Des Moines, Iowa.

In 1942, with all her added responsibilities, sixty-seven-year-old Bethune realized that she could not also fulfill her commitment as president of Bethune-Cookman College. She selected James Colston to take over the presidency. At a special meeting, she told the trustees, "You know of the prayers and the hardships, the joys and the sorrows that have gone into the building of this beautiful institution. There is nothing on earth so beautiful to me as this school. I have two children—my son, Albert, and Bethune-Cookman College. I gave birth to both of them and I love them with a devotion that can never die."[5] One year earlier, the Florida State Department of Education had approved a four-year college program for the school.

Bethune also averted a volatile situation in Detroit. Funds that had been earmarked for a housing project in a black area were being redirected to a white area.

Bethune and her son, Albert, share a quiet moment at home. On the wall is a portrait of Samuel and Patsy McLeod. Bert was their ninetieth grandchild!

Bethune met with her constant ally, Eleanor Roosevelt. As a result, the funds were sent to their intended destination, and the Sojourner Truth Housing Project was constructed.

Also in 1942, the Southern Conference for Human Welfare presented Bethune with its Thomas Jefferson Award. In 1943, Bethune received another title—general. The Women's Army for National Defense (WANDS), an all-black women's service organization, gave her this honor. On public occasions, Bethune would wear the uniform with the four stars on the shoulder.

Bethune persisted with her drive to employ black youth in the defense industries. In an essay, she wrote of the "frustrated efforts of Negroes to find a place in war production: the absolute denial of employment in many cases, or employment far below the level of their skills, numerous restrictions in their efforts to get training, [and the] resistance of labor unions to the improving and utilization of their skills on the job."[6]

One effective way to include black youths was the interstate transfer plan. After the youth were taught the skills they would need, they were transferred to areas with labor shortages. The largest such training project took place in Rocky Mount, North Carolina. There, 963 African-American males were trained for work in the Norfolk Navy Yard.[7]

By April 1943, blacks made up 20 percent of all

youth in the out-of-school work projects. Young African Americans particularly benefited from the Special Fund for Negroes, which aided black graduate students and black colleges. The fund assisted 4,118 students and more than one hundred black colleges with aid totaling $609,930.

Overall, more than sixty thousand black youths benefited from National Youth Administration programs.[8] Bethune helped set them up in both work study and out-of-school programs.

During its eight-year tenure, the NYA served several million young people at a cost of $685 million. But despite the NYA's successes, defense spending usurped the funds allocated for social programs. In July 1943, Congress ended the National Youth Administration.

Bethune's mission for racial justice and equality forged on. The beautiful beaches of Daytona Beach were marred by the ugliness of segregation: African Americans could enjoy the beaches only with a permit. In 1943, Bethune, along with some associates, purchased land for $200,000. The two-and-a-half-mile strip of oceanfront property was incorporated as Bethune-Volusia Beach. On this beach, no permit was required.

In 1943, under Bethune's leadership, the National Council of Negro Women purchased a house in Washington, D.C. Two years earlier, Bethune had solicited $10,000 from Marshall Field III for the down payment.

The new NCNW headquarters at 1318 Vermont Avenue N.W. would serve as more than office space and a meeting place. In those days, it was improper for a woman to check into a hotel alone. Therefore, the top-floor bedrooms would be used to lodge visiting female guests. The house also became Bethune's residence.

With Bethune at the helm, the NCNW persisted in its campaign for the inclusion of African-American women in the war effort. In 1944, the NCNW sponsored the S.S. *Harriet Tubman* liberty ship, which was the first ship named in honor of an African-American woman.

On April 12, 1945, America suffered a tragic loss when President Roosevelt died. Grief-stricken, Bethune attended his funeral in the East Room of the White House. In a radio broadcast, she spoke for all African Americans on his passing: "Today, we breathe a sigh—we wipe a tear—we are filled with remorse."[9]

The first lady presented Bethune with an engraved oak walking stick that had belonged to President Roosevelt.

Prior to the president's death, a conference had been scheduled in San Francisco for April 25, 1945, to draft a charter for the United Nations. This new organization would be dedicated to world peace and human dignity. Countries around the world hoped to use the lessons of the war to plan a blueprint for peace. The U.S. State Department selected Bethune to serve as an official consultant. The other two African-American consultants were W. E. B. Du Bois and Walter White of the NAACP. Bethune and her fellow consultants spoke out at the conference for the independence of the millions of people still under colonial rule in Africa and elsewhere in the world. Commenting on the conference, Bethune wrote: "The masses of the peoples of the world are demanding a major role in the shaping of the new civilization which began to dawn in San Francisco. The world tomorrow must be a 'people's world'—if our civilization is to survive."[10]

In 1947, after having filled in as president of Bethune-Cookman College for one year, seventy-two-year-old Bethune again resigned from the position. Dr. Richard V. Moore became the new president. Bethune remained on the board of trustees. Her numerous civic activities kept her very busy.

In 1948, Bethune began writing a weekly column for *The Chicago Defender*, the most influential black weekly newspaper of the time. Through her column, Bethune reached a national audience. Meanwhile, her accomplishments continued to be noted and celebrated. In 1949, Rollins College in Winter Park, Florida, awarded her an honorary doctorate degree. This was the first time a white southern college had bestowed such an honor on an African American. Bethune also visited Haiti at its president's invitation. There, President Dumarsais Estimé awarded her the Medal of Honor and Merit.

In 1949, Bethune resigned from the presidency of the National Council of Negro Women. She took on the honorary title of president-emeritus.

Of course, no one in the public eye can avoid being the occasional target of criticism. Rumors linked Bethune with Communists at a time when an impassioned fear of Communism was sweeping the country. In the 1950s, the United States and the Soviet Union were locked in competition, and many Americans feared that their way of life was being threatened by Communism—the Soviet system of government. Many distinguished Americans were falsely accused of being Communists and of trying to undermine the American way of life.

After Bethune was invited to speak at a meeting of the National Council on American-Soviet Friendship in New York, a Texas congressman accused her of being a Communist. In 1952, a school in Englewood, New Jersey, canceled an invitation for Bethune to speak because of her alleged Communist ties.

Members of the press as well as many prominent citizens rallied to Bethune's defense. Her longtime friend Eleanor Roosevelt, who wrote a daily newspaper column about important issues of the day, spoke out in Bethune's defense. In her column, "My Day," published in newspapers across the country, Roosevelt wrote, "If she did belong to any [Communist organizations], I am sure with her keen mind she soon discovered something wrong and was not a member for long. If she went to them to speak, she undoubtedly did them good."[11]

Bethune gave many speeches at schools and churches. Here, she speaks at a school graduation.

On a more positive note, a lifelong dream—to visit the continent of Africa—came true for Bethune that year. President Truman invited her to attend the second inaugural of President William Tubman of Liberia. There, she was awarded the Star of Africa by President Tubman. This is one of Liberia's highest honors.

During this time, Bethune also initiated a new project: the Mary McLeod Bethune Foundation. A $100,000 endowment fund was established to support the foundation. Eleanor Roosevelt was one of its earlier contributors. The foundation would carry on Bethune's legacy—creating a research institute, awarding scholarships, and promoting interracial goodwill.

Bethune also became involved with the Moral Re-Armament Movement of Dr. Frank N. D. Buchman. This movement aimed to unite people from around the world along four values: honesty, purity, unselfishness, and love. The organization opposed the apartheid policy of racial segregation in South Africa. In 1955, Bethune traveled to Switzerland for a conference, where in a speech she said, "I know you cannot all remember my name, but you will remember this face, remember this crown of white hair, remember the yearnings of a heart that is pleading for the unity of the world."[12]

On May 17, 1954, the Supreme Court issued a groundbreaking decision in the struggle for racial

Bethune spent the last days of her life at Bethune-Cookman College. She called her home there, above, the Retreat.

equality. In *Brown* v. *Board of Education of Topeka, Kansas*, the Court ruled that segregated public schools were unconstitutional. Bethune praised the decision in her column in *The Chicago Defender*:

> There can be no divided democracy, no class government, no half-free country, under the Constitution. . . . We are on our way. But these are frontiers which we must conquer, pushing our claims further. We must gain full equality in education, full equality in the franchise, full equality in economic opportunity, and full equality in the religious abundance of life.[13]

A year later, on May 18, 1955, Mary McLeod Bethune died of heart failure in her Florida home, the Retreat. She was buried behind the Retreat near her beloved Bethune-Cookman College.

Prior to her death, Bethune had published her last will and testament. For future generations, she had written these words:

> Sometimes I ask myself if I have any other legacy to leave. Truly, my worldly possessions are few. Yet, my experiences have been rich. Here, then is my legacy: I leave you love. . . . I leave you hope. . . . I leave you a thirst for education. . . . I leave you faith. . . . I leave you racial dignity. . . . I leave you a desire to live harmoniously with your fellow men. . . . I leave you finally a responsibility to our young people.[14]

10

LEGACIES

The legacy of Mary McLeod Bethune has continued in many ways long after her death. In 1974, a seventeen-foot-high bronze statue of Bethune was dedicated in Lincoln Park in Washington, D.C. Funds for the monument were raised by the National Council of Negro Women. It was the first monument to an African American or to a woman erected on public land in the nation's capital.

In 1985, the U.S. Postal Service issued a stamp in honor of Bethune. The stamp was part of the Black Heritage series.

In May 2000, the American Red Cross honored

Mary McLeod Bethune as a millennium hero. The first-ever Red Cross Millennium Hero Award was presented to the president of Bethune-Cookman College in honor of Bethune's humanitarian work and its continuation through the staff and students of the college.[1]

Today, the National Council of Negro Women thrives as a strong and significant organization. It includes thirty-eight national women's organizations; more than two hundred community-based chapters; more than twenty college-based chapters; and sixty-thousand individual members. The NCNW has a national headquarters in Washington, D.C., and maintains international field offices in Dakar (Senegal) and Cairo (Egypt). The NCNW is engaged in numerous projects across the nation and the world, with programs that provide food, educational opportunities, job training, child care, and awareness of HIV and sexually transmitted diseases.[2]

Another component of Bethune's rich legacy is the Mary McLeod Bethune Council House. The first headquarters of the NCNW, at 1318 Vermont Avenue N.W., Washington, D.C., is now open as a historical site run by the National Park Service. It commemorates the life of Bethune and the NCNW with a tour, exhibits, and a film. Also located there is the National Archives for Black Women's History. It is the only collection solely

"I cannot rest while there is a single Negro boy or girl lacking the chance to prove his worth," said Mary McLeod Bethune.

dedicated to the preservation of materials relating to African-American women.

Bethune's beloved Bethune-Cookman College still stands as the only remaining historically black college founded by an African-American woman. It is the sixth largest college of the forty-one-member United Negro College Fund (UNCF). The college offers bachelor's degrees in thirty-nine major areas, including business, education, and nursing. By June 2000, the college endowment was valued at more than $25 million—a monumental achievement for a school founded with $1.50.[3]

Also located on the college campus is the Mary McLeod Bethune Foundation, housed in the Retreat, where Bethune lived and died. The foundation has been designated as a National Historic Landmark by the National Park Service.

These legacies bear witness to the indelible mark that Mary McLeod Bethune has made on this nation and the world with her head, her hands, and her heart.

CHRONOLOGY

1875—Mary McLeod Bethune is born in Mayesville, South Carolina, on July 10.

1882—Attends the Mayesville Mission School.

1887—Leaves for Scotia Seminary in Concord, North Carolina.

1894—Attends Moody Bible Institute in Chicago.

1896—Teaches at Haines Normal and Industrial Institute, Augusta, Georgia.

1897—Teaches at the Kindell Institute, Sumter, South Carolina.

1898—Marries Albertus Bethune.

1899—Has her only child, Albert McLeod Bethune.

1904—Opens the Daytona Normal and Industrial Institute for Negro Girls in Daytona Beach, Florida, on October 3.

1907—Faith Hall is erected as the new home for the Daytona Institute; establishes the Tomako Mission.

1911—Opens the Patsy McLeod Hospital.

1914—Recruits African Americans for the Red Cross on a three-state tour.

1919—Husband, Albertus, dies.

1920—Mobilizes members of the African-American community to vote despite a showdown with the Ku Klux Klan.

1921—As president of the Florida Federation of Colored Women's Clubs, establishes a residence for delinquent black girls.

1923—The Daytona Normal and Industrial Institute merges with Cookman Institute to form Bethune-Cookman College.

1924—Is elected president of the National Association of Colored Women.

1927—Spends a four-month vacation in Europe; attends a luncheon at the home of Eleanor and Franklin Delano Roosevelt.

1928—Receives an invitation to the White House from President Calvin Coolidge; establishes a national headquarters for the NACW in Washington, D.C.; meets her benefactor, Mary Chrisman.

1935—Receives the Spingarn Medal from the NAACP; is appointed to the National Advisory Committee of the NYA; founds the National Council of Negro Women.

1936—Is appointed head of the NYA's Division of Negro Affairs; organizes the Black Cabinet.

1940—Breaks the color barrier at Johns Hopkins Hospital in Baltimore, Maryland.

1941—Bethune-Cookman College becomes a four-year liberal arts college.

1942—Is appointed special assistant to Lieutenant Colonel Oveta Culp Hobby of the Women's Army Auxiliary Corps.

1943—Is made an honorary general in the Women's

Army for National Defense; the headquarters of the NCNW is purchased; purchases Bethune-Volusia Beach.

1945—Gives a radio address as a representative of African Americans on the death of President Roosevelt; as a delegate, attends San Francisco conference to form the United Nations.

1949—Receives an honorary doctorate degree from Rollins College; receives the Medal of Honor and Merit from the president of Haiti.

1952—Attends the inauguration of President William Tubman in Liberia, Africa, and is awarded the Star of Africa.

1955—In Switzerland, gives a speech at the conference of the Moral Re-Armament Movement; dies on May 18.

1974—A bronze statue of Bethune is erected in Lincoln Park, Washington, D.C.—the first monument to an African American or a woman in the nation's capital.

Chapter Notes

Chapter 1. "But We Voted!"
1. Rackham Holt, *Mary McLeod Bethune* (New York: Doubleday & Co. Inc., 1964), p. 120.
2. Walter Russell Bowie, *Women of Light* (New York: Harper & Row, Inc., 1963), p. 125.
3. Ibid.

Chapter 2. The Girl Who Wanted to Read
1. Gerda Lerner, ed., *Black Women in White America* (New York: Vintage Books, 1992), p. 135.
2. Herbert G. Gutman, *The Black Family in Slavery and Freedom, 1750–1925* (New York: Pantheon Books, 1976), pp. 9–12.
3. John Hope Franklin, *From Slavery to Freedom* (New York: Alfred A. Knopf, 1988), pp. 223–227.
4. Rackham Holt, *Mary McLeod Bethune* (New York: Doubleday & Co., Inc., 1964), p. 7.
5. <http://fpc.dos.state.fl.us/learning/Bethune/documents/interview.html> (August 20, 2000).
6. Edwin R. Embree, *13 Against the Odds* (New York: Viking Press, 1944), p. 11.
7. Holt, p. 19.
8. Embree, p. 11.
9. Holt, p. 24.
10. <http://fpc.dos.state.fl.us/learning/Bethune/documents/interview.html> (August 20, 2000).

Chapter 3. A New Mission
1. <http://fpc.dos.state.fl.us/learning/Bethune/documents/interview.html> (November 23, 2001).

2. "Total Student Development" brochure from Barber-Scotia College, Concord, North Carolina, 2001.

3. Rackham Holt, *Mary McLeod Bethune* (New York: Doubleday & Co. Inc., 1964), p. 40.

4. Walter Russell Bowie, *Women of Light* (New York: Harper & Row, Inc., 1963), p. 122.

5. Mary McLeod Bethune Papers: The Bethune Foundation Collection, John H. Bracey, Jr., and August Meier, eds. (Bethesda, Md.: University Publications of America, 1996), p. 6.

6. Amy Alexander, *Fifty Black Women Who Changed America* (Secaucus, N.J.: Carol Publishing Group, 1999), p. 46.

Chapter 4. Head, Hand, and Heart

1. Edwin R. Embree, *13 Against the Odds* (New York: Viking Press, 1944), p. 15.

2. Mary McLeod Bethune, "Faith That Moved a Dump Heap," *Who, the Magazine about People*, June 1941, p. 34.

3. Allen W. Jones, "The Role of Tuskegee Institute in the Education of Black Farmers," *Journal of Negro History*, April 1975, pp. 160–165.

4. Mary McLeod Bethune Papers: The Bethune Foundation Collection, John H. Bracey, Jr., and August Meier, eds. (Bethesda, Md.: University Publications of America, 1996), p. 34.

5. Audrey Thomas McCluskey, *Mary McLeod Bethune and the Education of Black Girls in the South, 1904–1923* (Bloomington: Indiana University, 1991), p. 174.

6. Gerda Lerner, ed., *Black Women in White America* (New York: Vintage Books, 1992), p. 138.

7. Ibid., p. 139.

8. Roy E. Finkenbine, "'Our Little Circle': Benevolent Reformers, the Slater Fund, and the Argument for Black Industrial Education, 1882–1908,"

in Donald G. Nieman, ed., *African Americans and Education in the South, 1865–1900* (New York: Garland Publishing, 1994), vol. 10, pp. 70–71.

9. Sadie Iola Daniel, *Women Builders* (Washington, D.C.: Associated Publishers, Inc., 1931), p. 86.

Chapter 5. Bethune-Cookman College

1. Herbert Aptheker, ed., *A Documentary History of the Negro People in the United States, 1933–1945* (New York: Carol Publishing Group, 1992), p. 106.

2. Rackham Holt, *Mary McLeod Bethune* (New York: Doubleday & Co. Inc., 1964), p. 92.

3. Jeanne Noble, *Beautiful, Also, Are the Souls of My Black Sisters* (New Jersey: Prentice-Hall, Inc., 1978), p. 139.

4. Audrey Thomas McCluskey, *Mary McLeod Bethune and the Education of Black Girls in the South, 1904–1923* (Bloomington: Indiana University, 1991), p. 188.

5. Gerda Lerner, ed., *Black Women in White America* (New York: Vintage Books, 1992), p. 142.

6. McCluskey, p. 106.

7. Catherine Owens Peare, *Mary McLeod Bethune* (New York: Vanguard Press, 1951), p. 124.

8. *Afro-American Encyclopedia*, vol. 1 (North Miami: Educational Book Publishers, Inc., 1974), p. 250.

Chapter 6. The Black Rose

1. Darlene Clark Hine, ed., *Black Women in America* (New York: Facts on File, Inc., 1997), p. 54.

2. Mary McLeod Bethune Papers, The Bethune Foundation Collection, n.d.

3. Rackham Holt, *Mary McLeod Bethune* (New York: Doubleday & Co. Inc., 1964), p. 166.

4. Florence Johnson Hicks, *Mary McLeod Bethune* (Washington, D.C.: Nuclassics and Science Publishing Co., 1975), p. 41.

5. "Mrs. Bethune Tells of Effect of Intense Hurricane Storm on Florida's Negro People," *Birmingham Reporter*, September 29, 1928, p. 142.

6. <http://womenshistory.about.com/library/qu/blqubeth.html> (February 25, 2002).

Chapter 7. National Council of Negro Women

1. Jeanne Noble, *Beautiful, Also, Are the Souls of My Black Sisters* (Englewood Cliffs, N.J.: Prentice-Hall, Inc., 1978), p. 140.

2. Paul Giddings, *When and Where I Enter* (New York: William Morrow and Co., Inc., 1984), p. 207.

3. Darlene Clark Hine, ed., *Black Women in America* (New York: Facts on File, Inc., 1997), p. 52.

4. Mary McLeod Bethune Papers, 1923–1942, Amistad Research Center, New Orleans, Louisiana.

5. Giddings, p. 211.

6. Ibid., p. 212.

7. Mary McLeod Bethune, "My Secret Talks with FDR," *Ebony*, April 1949, p. 57.

8. Ibid., p. 59.

Chapter 8. Bethune and the Black Cabinet

1. Nancy J. Weiss, *Farewell to the Party of Lincoln* (Princeton, N.J.: Princeton University Press, 1983), p. 137.

2. Mabel E. Deutrich and Virginia C. Purdy, eds., *Clio Was a Woman: Studies in the History of American Women* (Washington, D.C.: Howard University Press, 1980), p. 156.

3. Mary McLeod Bethune, "My Secret Talks with FDR," *Ebony*, April 1949, p. 60.

4. Paula Giddings, *When and Where I Enter* (New York: Doubleday & Co. Inc., 1964), p. 229.

5. Rackham Holt, *Mary McLeod Bethune* (New York: Doubleday & Co., Inc., 1964), p. 218.

6. Herbert Aptheker, *A Documentary History of the Negro People in the United States, 1933–1945* (New York: Carol Publishing Group, 1992), pp. 55–60.

7. B. Joyce Ross, "Mary McLeod Bethune and the National Youth Administration," *The Journal of Negro History*, January 1975, p. 12.

8. Mary Frances Berry, "Twentieth Century Black Women in Education," *The Journal of Negro Education*, Summer 1982, p. 291.

Chapter 9. "I Leave You Love"

1. "Politics and Public Issues," pp. 241, 244, Mary McLeod Bethune Papers, Mary McLeod Bethune Foundation, August 1941.

2. Executive Order 8802, <http://www.civilrights. org> (November 24, 2001).

3. "Mrs. Bethune Protests to Secretary Stimson," *Atlanta Daily World*, October 19, 1942.

4. Mabel E. Deutrich and Virginia C. Purdy, eds., *Clio Was a Woman: Studies in the History of American Women* (Washington, D.C.: Howard University Press, 1980), p. 167.

5. James C. Colston Papers, Bethune-Cookman College Archives, December 15, 1942

6. Rayford W. Logan, *What the Negro Wants* (Chapel Hill: The University of North Carolina Press, 1944), p. 251.

7. Deutrich and Purdy., p. 168.

8. Ibid., p. 166.

9. Florence Johnson Hicks, *Mary McLeod Bethune* (Washington, D.C.: Nuclassics and Science Publishing Co., 1975), p. 32.

10. "Politics and Public Issues," p. 253, Mary McLeod Bethune Papers, Mary McLeod Bethune Foundation, June 1945.

11. <http://www.pbs.org/wgbh/amex/eleanor/ peopleevents/pande05.html> (November 23, 2001).

12. Hicks, p. 44.

13. Rackham Holt, *Mary McLeod Bethune* (New York: Doubleday & Co., Inc., 1964), p. 277.

14. "My Last Will and Testament," *Ebony*, August 1955.

Chapter 10. Legacies

1. Michelle Thompson, "American Red Cross Honors Dr. Mary McLeod Bethune as a Millennium Hero," <http://www.redcross.org/news/archives/2000/ 5-2-00.html> (February 25, 2002).

2. <http://www.ncnw.com/ncnwlegacy/aboutus/ htm> (November 24, 2001).

3. "Bethune/Cookman College," <http://www. volusiaflaglerhighered.org/aboutbcc.html> (February 25, 2002).

Further Reading

Bennett, Carolyn LaDelle. *An Annotated Bibliography of Mary McLeod Bethune's "Chicago Defender" Columns: 1948–1955*. Lewiston, N.Y.: Edwin Mellen Press, 2001.

Halasa, Malu. *Mary McLeod Bethune*. New York: Chelsea House Publishers, 1989.

McCluskey, Audrey Thomas, and Elaine M. Smith, eds. *Mary McLeod Bethune: Building a Better World, Essays and Selected Letters*. Bloomington: Indiana University Press, 2002.

Meltzer, Milton. *Mary McLeod Bethune: Voice of Black Hope*. New York: Puffin Books, 1987.

Poole, Bernice A. *Mary McLeod Bethune: Educator*. Los Angeles, Calif.: Holloway House, 1994.

Wilson, Beth P. *Giants for Justice: Bethune, Randolph, and King*. New York: Harcourt Brace Jovanovich, 1978.

Wolfe, Rinna Evelyn. *Mary McLeod Bethune*. New York: Franklin Watts, 1992.

INTERNET ADDRESSES

Mary McLeod Bethune Council House
<http://www.nps.gov/mamc/bethune/meet/frame.htm>

Bethune-Cookman College
<http://www.cookman.edu/Welcome/Founder/founder.
htm>

National Women's Hall of Fame
<http://www.greatwomen.org/women.php?action=
viewone&id=18>

National Council of Negro Women, Inc.
<http://www.ncnw.org/history.htm>

INDEX

Page numbers for photographs are in **boldface** type.